Science Questions

Why Does the Sun Shine?

by Rebecca Pettiford

Bullfrog Books

Ideas for Parents and Teachers

Bullfrog Books let children practice reading informational text at the earliest reading levels. Repetition, familiar words, and photo labels support early readers.

Before Reading

• Discuss the cover photo. What does it tell them?

• Look at the picture glossary together. Read and discuss the words.

Read the Book

• "Walk" through the book and look at the photos. Let the child ask questions. Point out the photo labels.

• Read the book to the child, or have him or her read independently.

After Reading

• Prompt the child to think more. Ask: The Sun makes heat and light. Why do people, plants, and animals need heat and light?

Bullfrog Books are published by Jump!
5357 Penn Avenue South
Minneapolis, MN 55419
www.jumplibrary.com

Library of Congress Cataloging-in-Publication Data

Names: Pettiford, Rebecca, author.
Title: Why does the sun shine? / by Rebecca Pettiford.
Description: Minneapolis, MN: Jump!, Inc., [2023]
Series: Science questions | Includes index.
Audience: Ages 5–8
Identifiers: LCCN 2022011509 (print)
LCCN 2022011510 (ebook)
ISBN 9798885240567 (hardcover)
ISBN 9798885240574 (paperback)
ISBN 9798885240581 (ebook)
Subjects: LCSH: Science—Miscellanea—Juvenile literature.
Classification: LCC Q163 .P493 2023 (print)
LCC Q163 (ebook)
DDC 523.7—dc23/eng20220517
LC record available at
https://lccn.loc.gov/2022011509
LC ebook record available at
https://lccn.loc.gov/2022011510

Editor: Jenna Gleisner
Designer: Emma Bersie

Photo Credits: Pasko Maksim/Shutterstock, cover; Aphelleon/Shutterstock, 1, 12–13 (Sun); G.roman/Shutterstock, 3; Josu Ozkaritz/Shutterstock, 4; Rawpixel.com/Shutterstock, 5; AlexLMX/iStock, 6–7, 23tl, 23tr; vmdesign.video/Shutterstock, 8–9, 23br; CeltStudio/Shutterstock, 10–11; Ivan Remitski/Dreamstime, 12–13 (Earth); Sunny Forest/Shutterstock, 14; Rezus/iStock, 15, 23bl; Peerapat Lekkla/Shutterstock, 16–17; Kuttelvaserova Stuchelova/Shutterstock, 18; Dennis W Donohue/Shutterstock, 19; Sergey Novikov/Shutterstock, 20–21; Jemastock/Shutterstock, 22; 19 STUDIO/Shutterstock, 24 (top), 24 (bottom).

Printed in the United States of America at Corporate Graphics in North Mankato, Minnesota.

Table of Contents

Ball of Gas

The Sun shines on Bella.

The Sun keeps us warm.

Sun

Earth

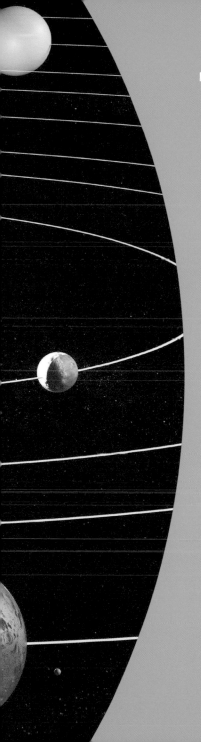

The Sun is in outer space.
Earth spins around it.
Other planets do, too.

The Sun is a big star.

It is made of hot gas.

It makes light
and heat.

The Sun shines.

It shines on Earth!

Earth spins.

Only the side that faces the Sun gets light.

On that side, it is day.

On the other, it is night!

night

day

The Sun is far away.

ray

But its rays are strong.
They reach Earth.

We need the Sun to live.
Plants need its heat
and light.

It helps them grow.

Many animals eat plants.

They need them to live.

grass ·····▶

Animals need the Sun, too!
It keeps them warm.

We play in the Sun!

Light and Heat

The Sun is a star. It is made of hot gas. It creates light and heat. It shines on Earth. Take a look!

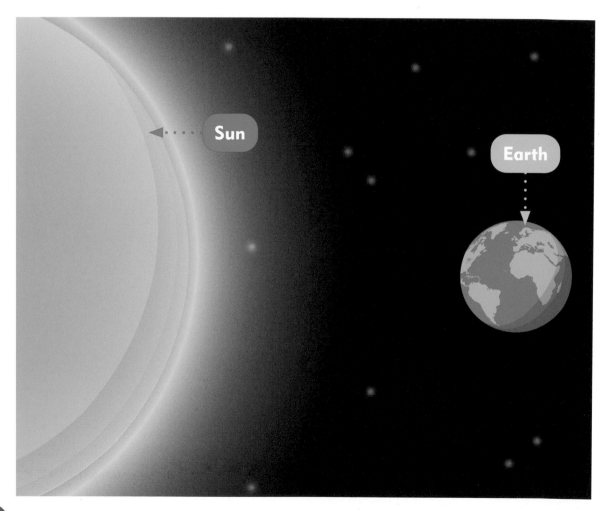

Picture Glossary

outer space
The universe beyond Earth.

planets
Large, round objects in outer space that circle the Sun.

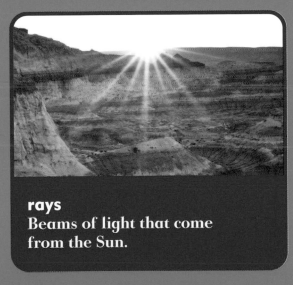

rays
Beams of light that come from the Sun.

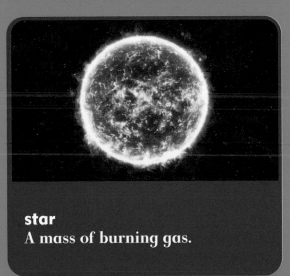

star
A mass of burning gas.

Index

To Learn More

Finding more information is as easy as 1, 2, 3.

❶ Go to www.factsurfer.com

❷ Enter "whydoestheSunshine" into the search box.

❸ Choose your book to see a list of websites.